MW01153506

THIS BOOK WILL BE CUT TO SHREDS BY:

_____

BOOKS THAT MAKE YOU SMILE

SQUARE ROOT OF SQUID PUBLISHING

Copyright © 2020 Square Root of Squid Publishing

All rights reserved. No part of this publication may be reproduced, distributed, or transmitted in any form or by any means, including photocopying, recording, or other electronic or mechanical methods, without the prior written permission of the publisher, except in the case of brief quotations embodied in critical reviews and certain other noncommercial uses permitted by copyright law.

WHAT YOU NEED

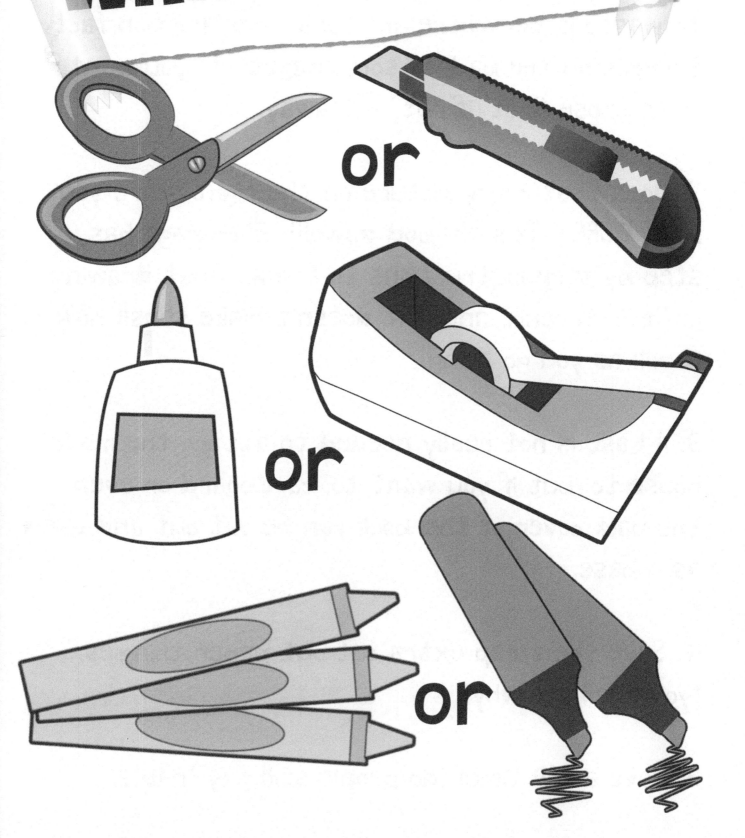

or

or

or

HOW TO USE THIS BOOK

1. A lot of the pages will be cut up, so in order not to waste paper there are some construction fact thingies on the back of some pages. If you want, read those first, if not, cut away.

2. Does that crazy picture on the right scare you? DON'T WORRY, It's all good dawg!!! Each page has step by step instructions to follow. That drawing is for reference and if it doesn't make sense now, it will as you go along.

3. A base is not really needed to attach the model house to, but if you want to, cardboard or even the back cover of this book can be cut out and used as a base.

4. Save the scrap extra cut out paper thingies. (you shall see why)

5. Have a RAD time! (do people still say "rad"?)

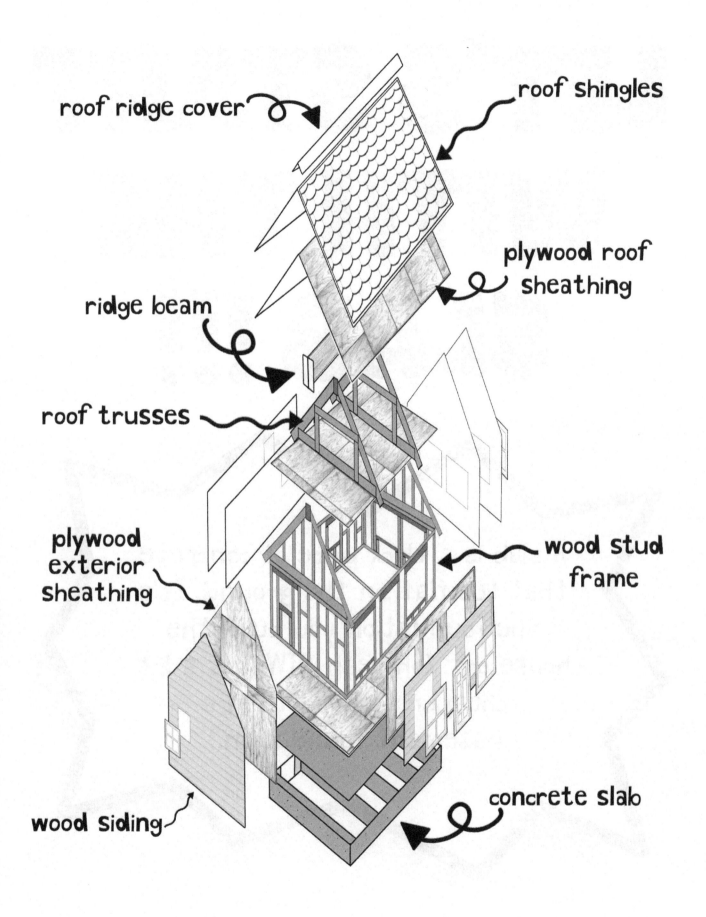

roof ridge cover

roof shingles

ridge beam

plywood roof sheathing

roof trusses

plywood exterior sheathing

wood stud frame

wood siding

concrete slab

LET'S START WITH THE SLAB !!!

A slab is a thick piece of concrete that lies flat on the ground. It's the foundation you build the house on. (oh yeah, BTW, it's a lot cheaper to build than a basement foundation.)

SLAB ASSEMBLY

STEP 4.
Cut up all the scrap paper and put it in between the rebars as aggregate.

STEP 1.
Cut out the slab and glue it into a box shape.

STEP 2.
Cut out and glue together the rebars.

subfloor

top slab

STEP 3.
Glue the rebars in place.

STEP 5.
Glue on the top slab and then glue on the subfloor.

WHAT ARE THE 3 MAIN TYPES OF FOUNDATIONS?

ANSWER

Slab

Basement

Crawlspace

cut
small
dotted
line

cut
small
dotted
line

cut
small
dotted
line

cut
small
dotted
line

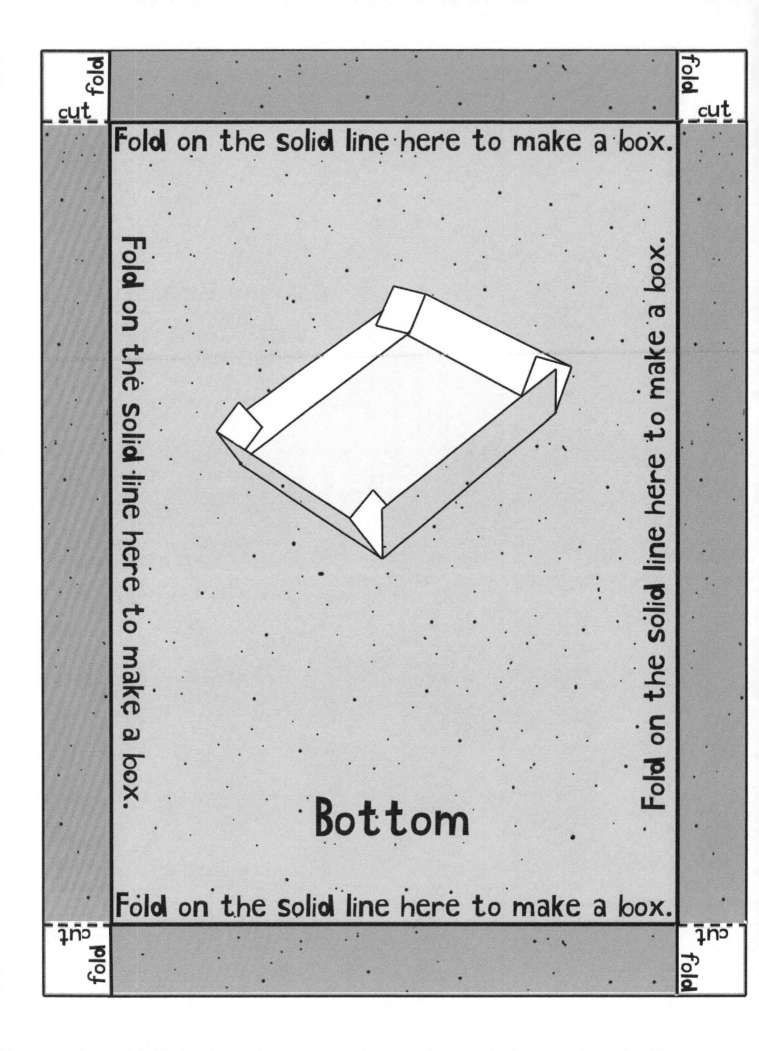

cut
fold
fold
cut
fold
cut

Fold on the solid line here to make a box.

Fold on the solid line here to make a box.

Fold on the solid line here to make a box.

Bottom

Fold on the solid line here to make a box.

cut
fold
cut
fold

LET'S MAKE ^paper REBAR

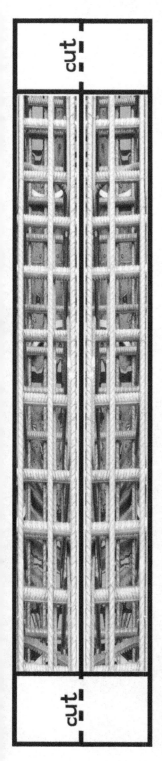

Within the cut-out strips:
cut ... cut ... cut ... cut

glue together

Cut those guys out and cut the small dotted lines. Fold in half and glue together with the flaps sticking out.

WHAT'S REBAR?
rebars are metal tubes that go in concrete to make it strong

SAVE THE SCRAP PAPER

MORE ~paper~ REBAR

Glue the rebar into position like this.

HOW IS A WOOD HOUSE ATTACHED TO THE FOUNDATION?

ANSWER

A wood sill plate has holes drilled in it and it goes on top of bolts in the concrete and is bolted down, the frame is attached to that sill plate.

ADD AGGREGATE

Cut all the paper scraps up and put the pieces in between the rebars as aggregate.

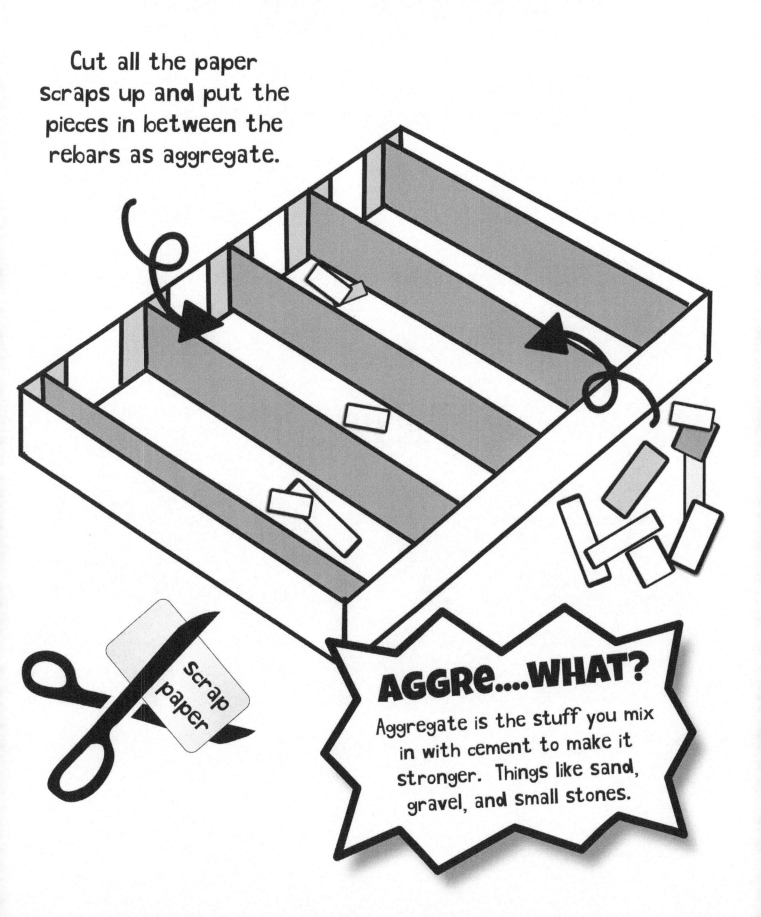

scrap paper

AGGRe....WHAT?

Aggregate is the stuff you mix in with cement to make it stronger. Things like sand, gravel, and small stones.

WHAT DOES CONCRETE CURING MEAN?

ANSWER

Curing is the hardening process of the concrete.

TOP SLAB

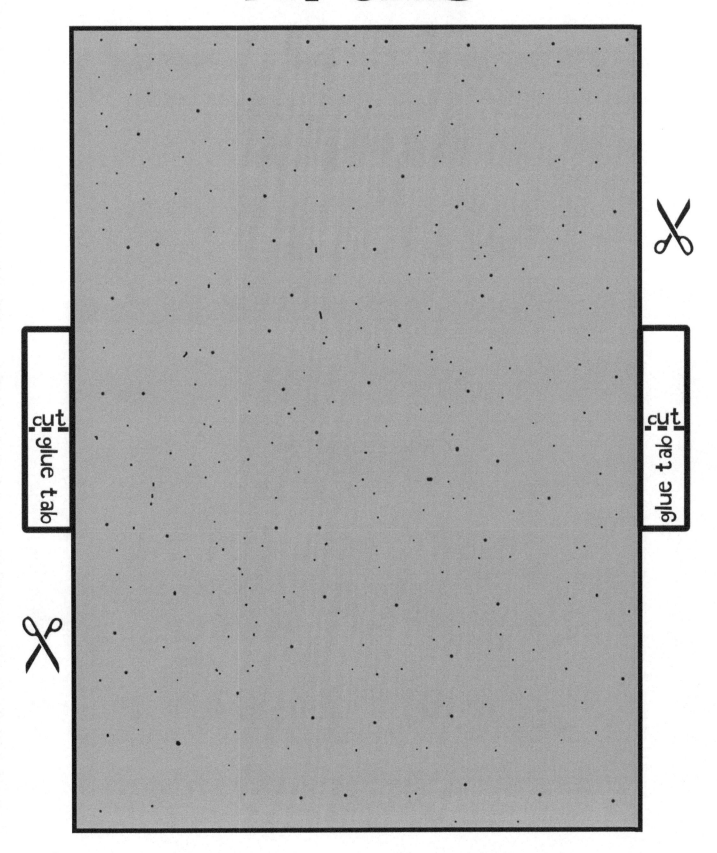

Cut out and glue on top of slab walls.

HOW DO YOU MAKE CONCRETE?

ANSWER

You make concrete by mixing cement, water, and aggregate together.

THE SUBFLOOR

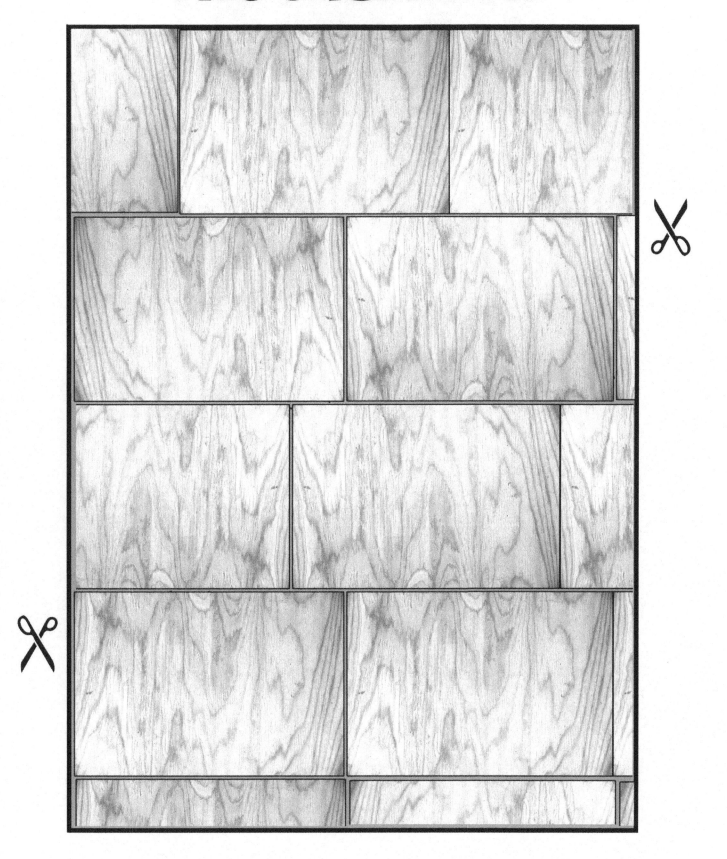

Cut out and glue on top of top slab.

WHAT'S A SUBFLOOR?

ANSWER

A subfloor is usually made of plywood or particle board. It is used to stick the finished floor to .

NEXT, LET'S BUILD THE HOUSE FRAME

Check out the floor plan on the next page to see where the walls go.

Think of the frame as the skeleton of the house. It holds everything together but is a lot less scary than a real skeleton. BOO!

THE FLOOR PLAN

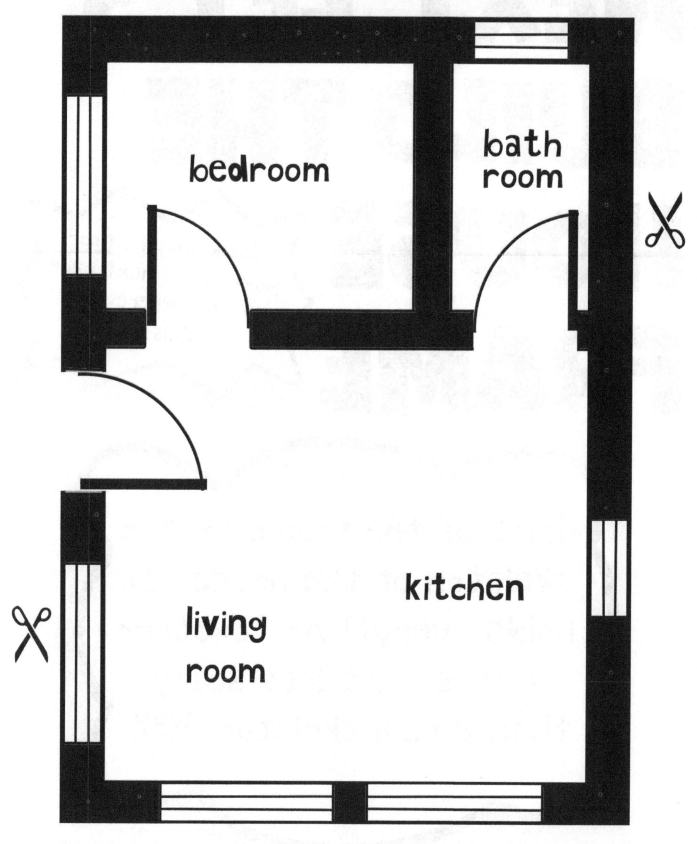

Cut this out and glue over the top slab. This will help to know where the walls go.

FRONT WALL FRAME
(inside)

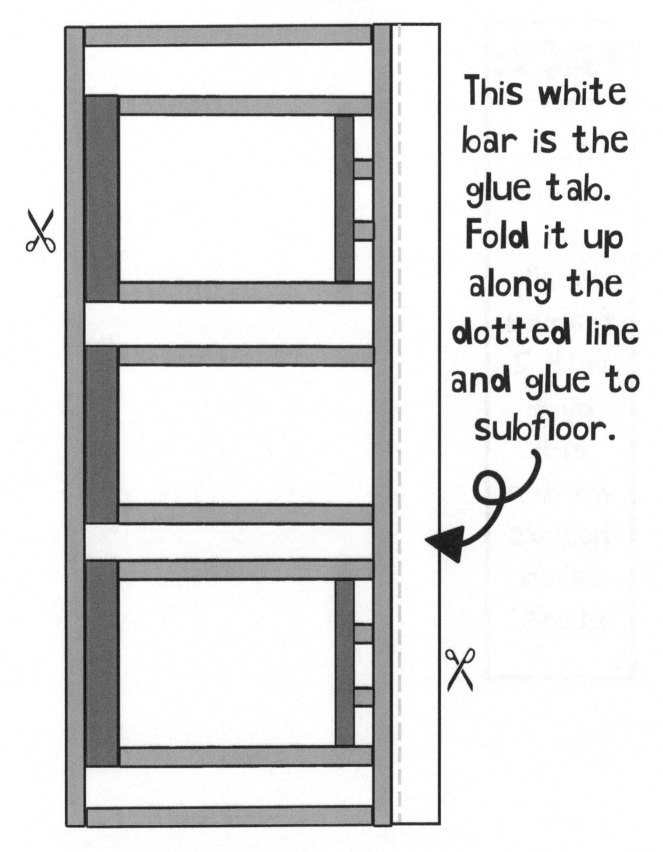

This white bar is the glue tab. Fold it up along the dotted line and glue to subfloor.

FRONT WALL FRAME
(outside)

FACT:

Wood houses are usually framed with 2 by 4 inch wooden boards called "studs".

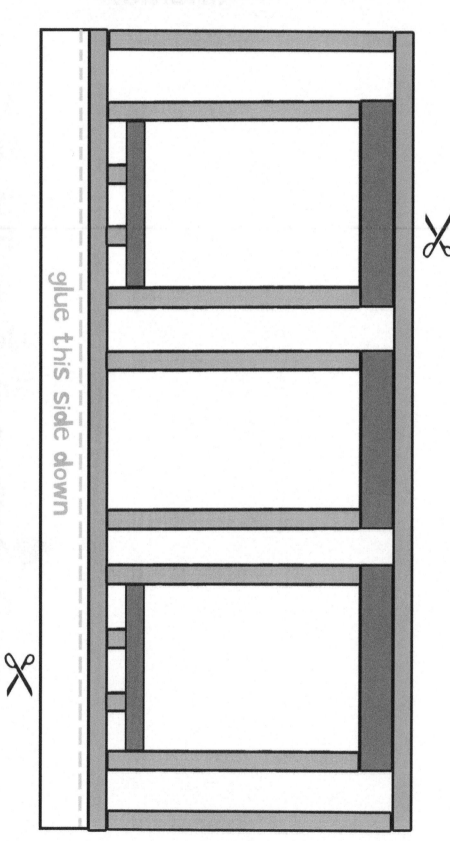

glue this side down

BACK WALL FRAME
(inside)

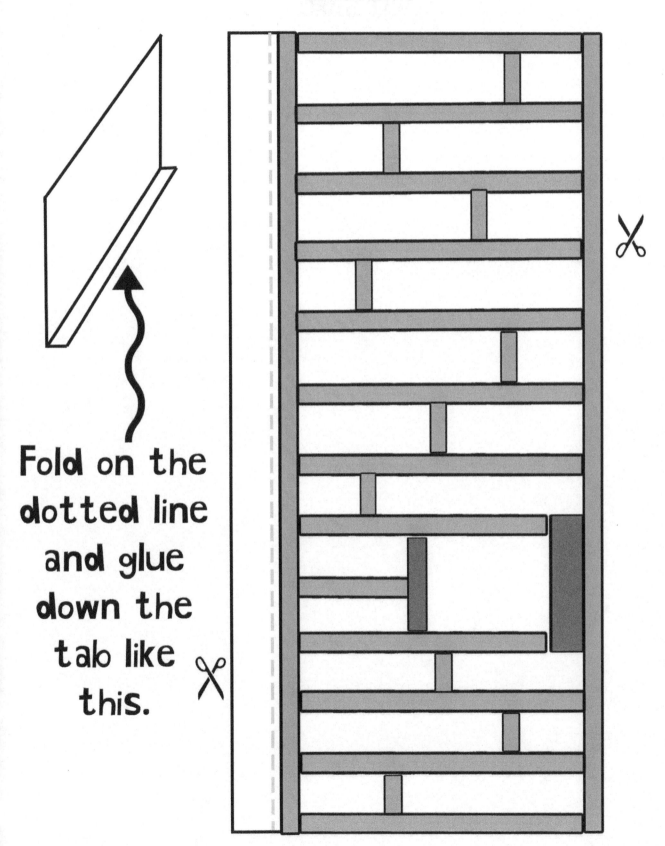

Fold on the dotted line and glue down the tab like this.

BACK WALL FRAME
(outside)

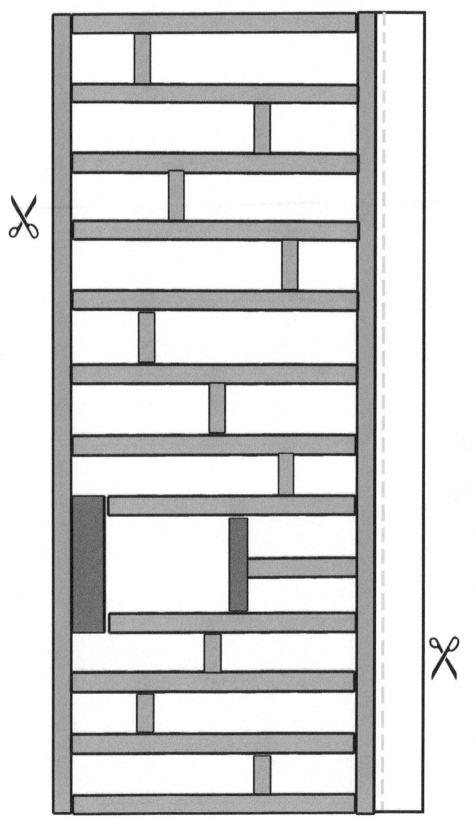

RIGHT SIDE WALL FRAME
(inside)

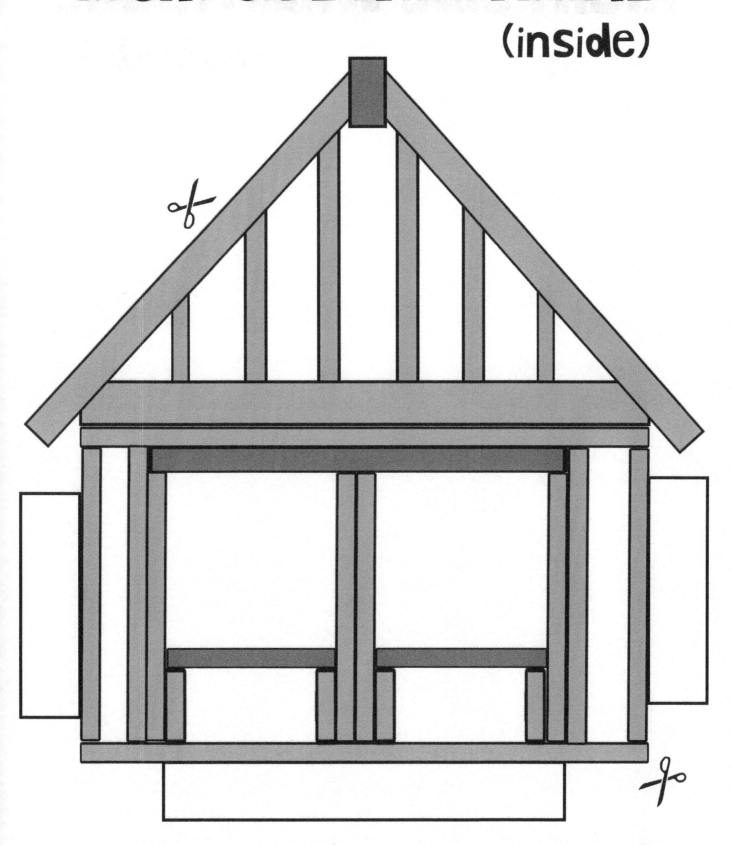

Cut out and glue the tabs to the floor and the walls.

RIGHT SIDE WALL FRAME
(outside)

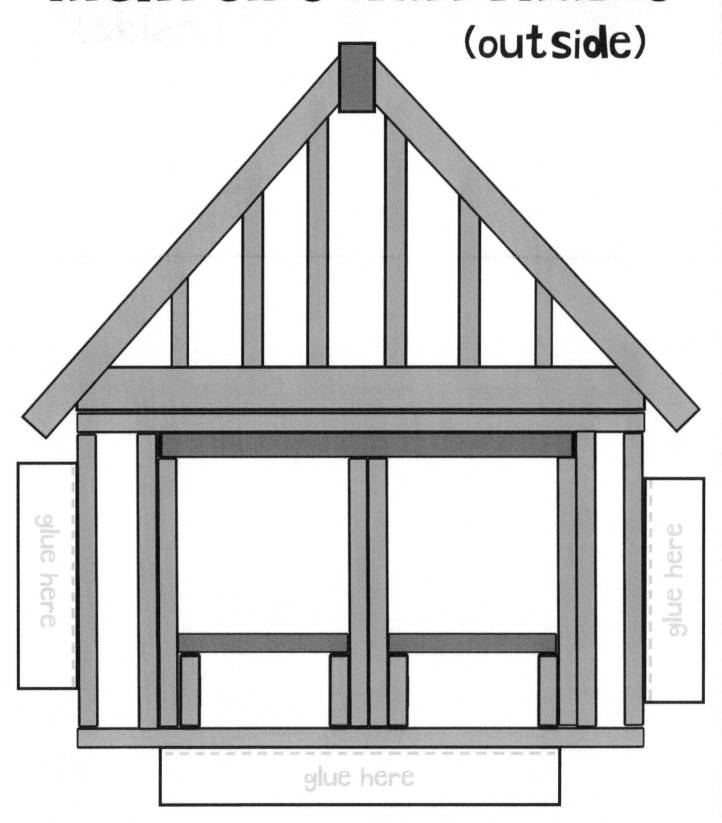

glue here

glue here

glue here

Fold tabs along the grey dotted lines and glue.

LEFT SIDE WALL FRAME
(inside)

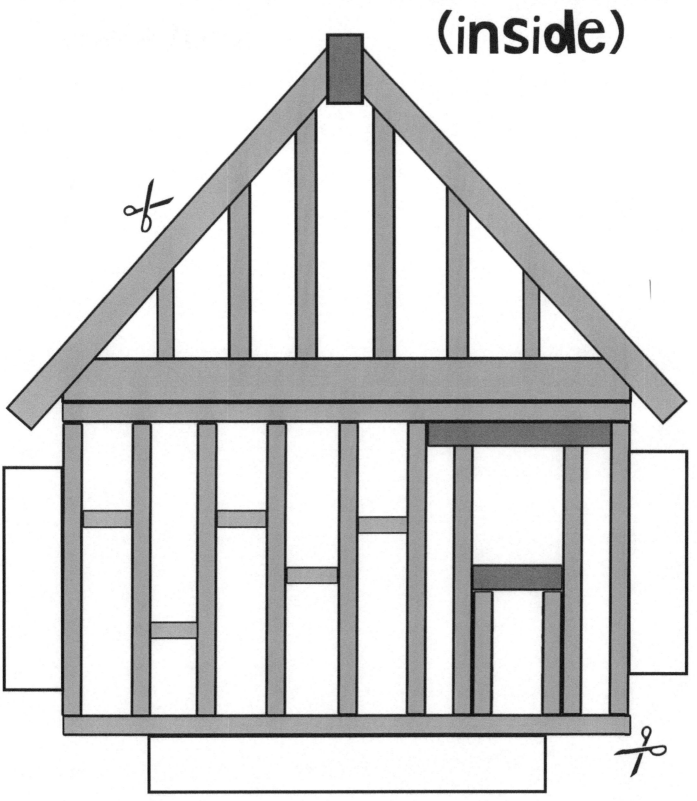

Cut out and glue the tabs to the floor and the walls.

LEFT SIDE WALL FRAME
(outside)

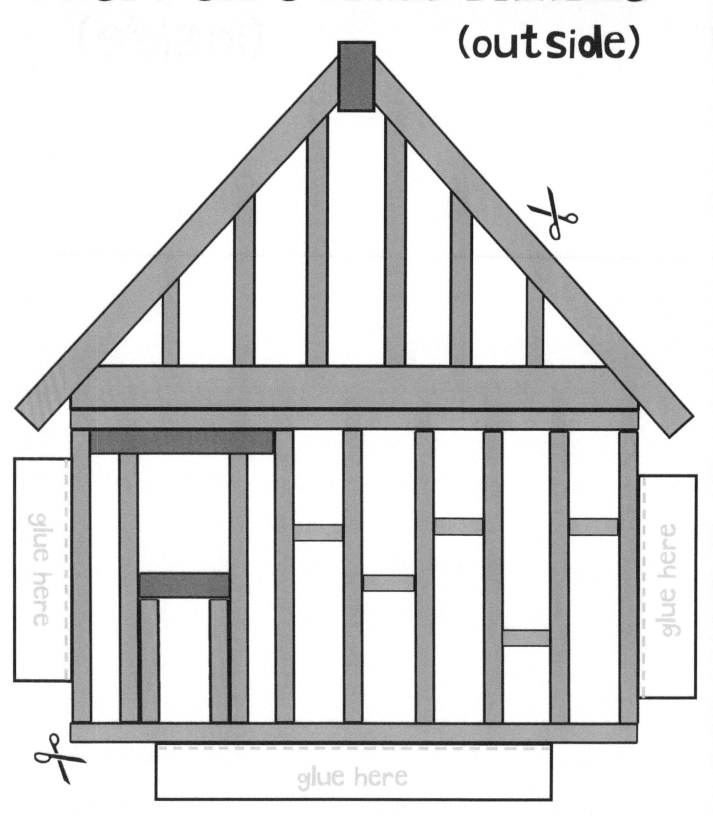

glue here

glue here

glue here

Fold tabs along the grey dotted lines and glue.

INTERIOR WALL FRAMES

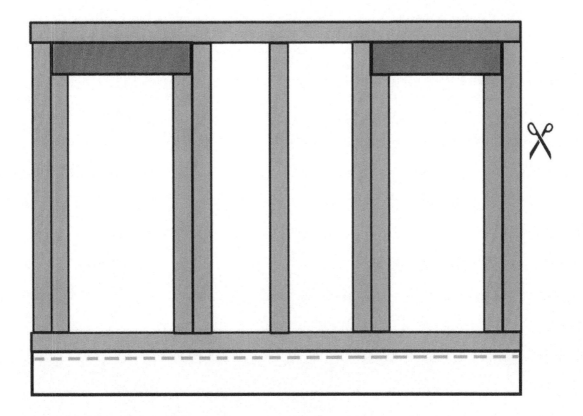

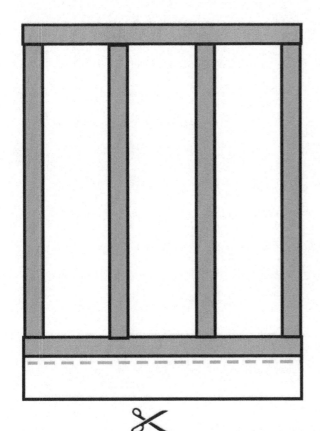

Cut out, fold on the dotted line and glue the frames in place according to the floor plan.

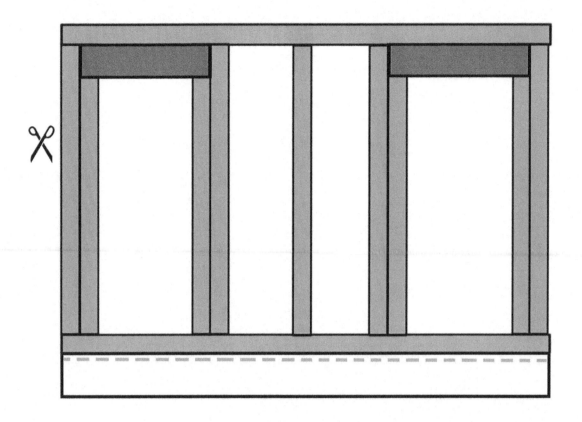

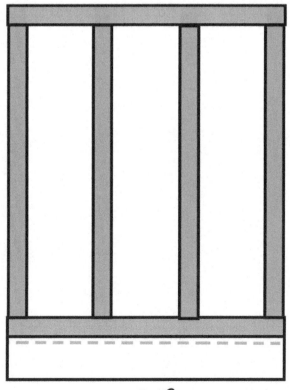

LET'S TALK
HEADERS & SILLS

Headers go over doors and windows so all the heavy weight above doesn't rest on the doors and windows.

Sills hold some of the weight of the window and give structure to the frame.

TIME TO ADD THE DRYWALL

Cut out the drywall and glue it together like this.

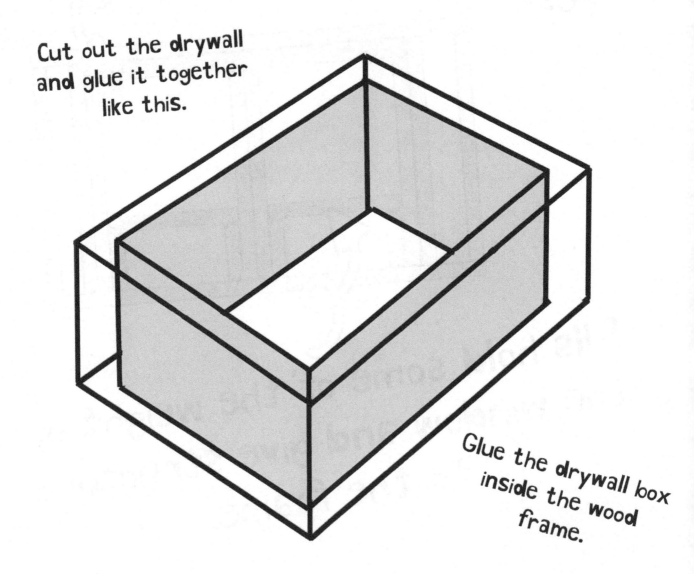

Glue the drywall box inside the wood frame.

DRYWALL

is a board that's put over **studs** to make a wall. It's like a **sandwich** with paper being the bread and gypsum being the meat.

left side

glue tab

cut slot for wall

glue tab

right side

glue tab

glue tab

Cut these guys out and glue the tabs to front and back **drywall** to make a rectangle.

WHAT WAS USED BEFORE DRYWALL?

ANSWER

Mostly plaster. It was mixed with animal hair to make it stronger. Argh! My wall has fleas!!!

DRYWALL

back

front

glue tab

glue tab

glue tab

glue tab

Cut out drywall, fold on dotted line, and glue
together with side panels to make a rectangle.

WHEN WAS DRYWALL INVENTED?

ANSWER

Drywall was invented in 1916 by The United States Gypsum Corporation.

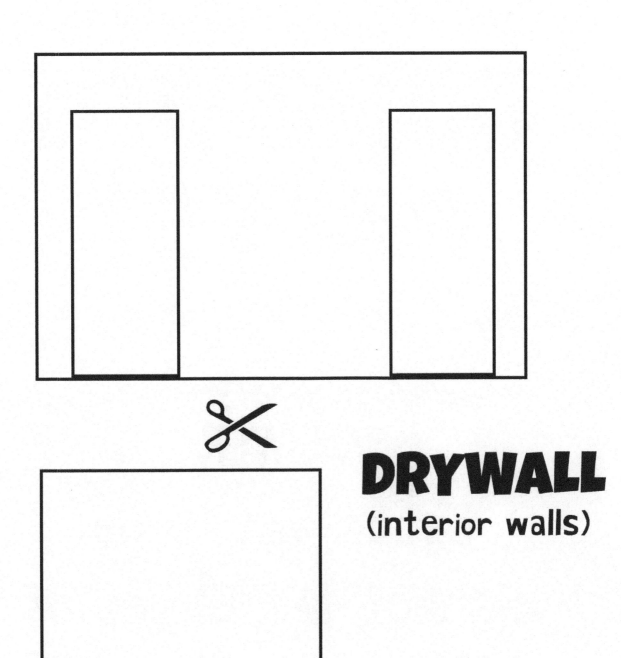

DRYWALL
(interior walls)

Cut 'em out and
glue 'em on.

WHAT ARE BATTS?

ANSWER

Batts are large blanket-like pieces of fiberglass insulation.

INSULATION

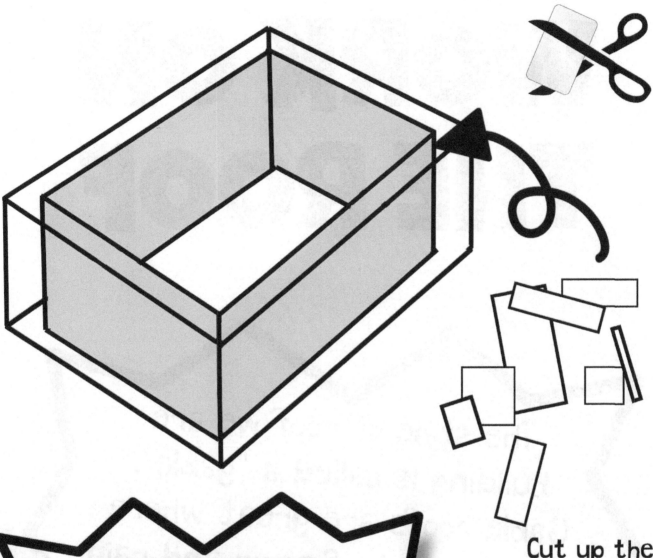

INSULATION

Insulation goes in the walls and ceilings to keep the house cozy warm in the winter and cool in the summer.

Cut up the paper scraps for insulation and fill up the space between the drywall and frame wall.

NOW LET'S WORK ON THE ROOF

The style of roof we are building is called a "gable". Gable roofs are great where there is a lot of snow and rain 'cause it let's the snow and rain fall off easily.

ROOF FLOOR

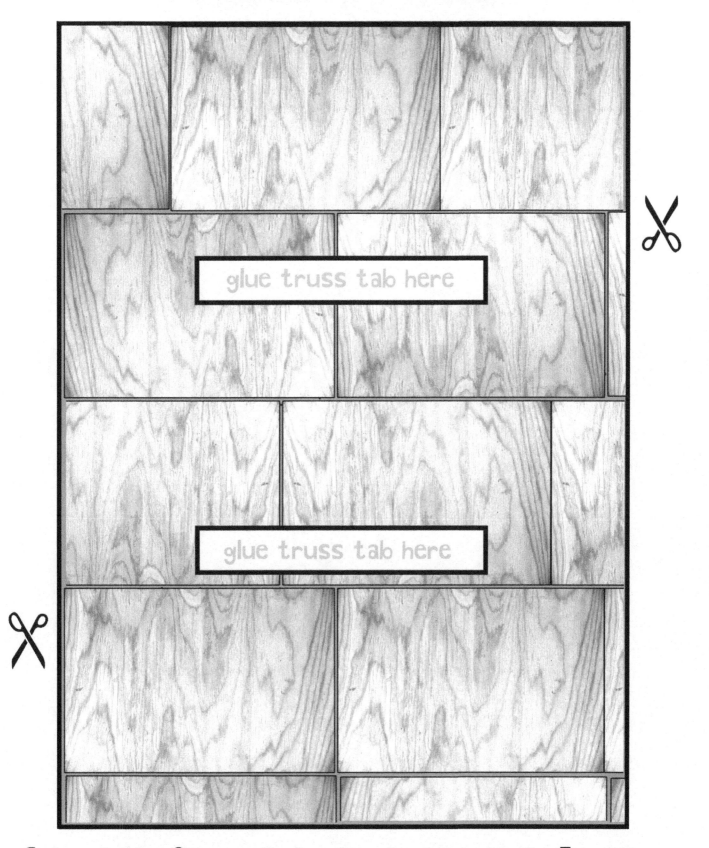

glue truss tab here

glue truss tab here

Cut out the floor and glue the trusses to it. The other
side of this floor will be the drywall ceiling.

DRYWALL CEILING

ROOF TRUSSES

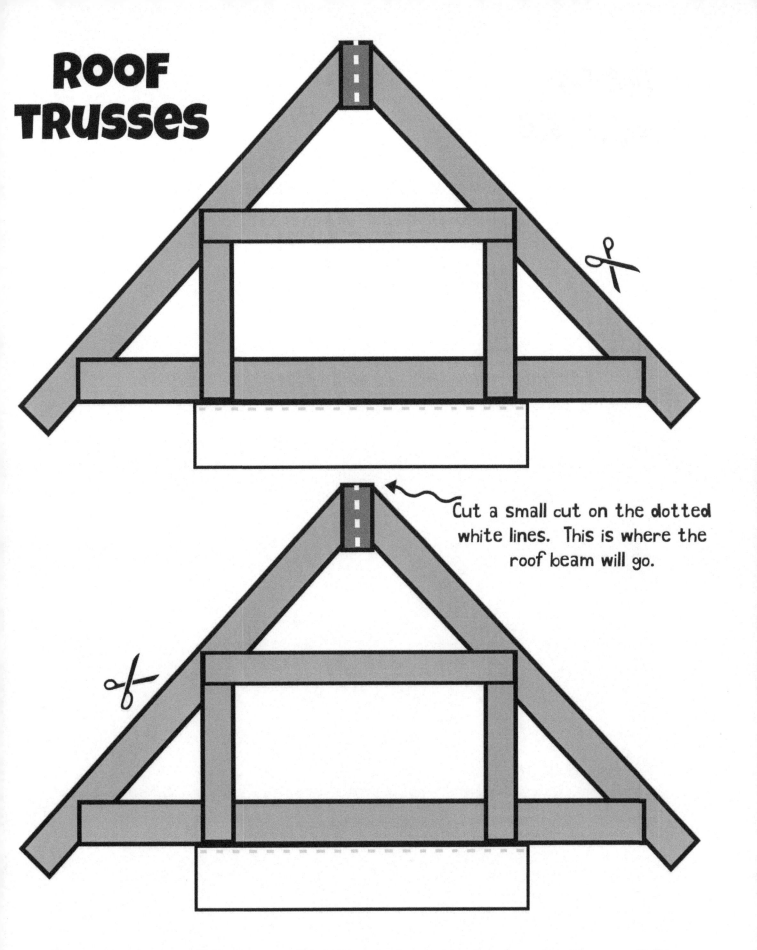

Cut a small cut on the dotted white lines. This is where the roof beam will go.

Cut out the roof trusses, fold the tabs and glue 'em to the roof floor.

ROOF TRUSSES

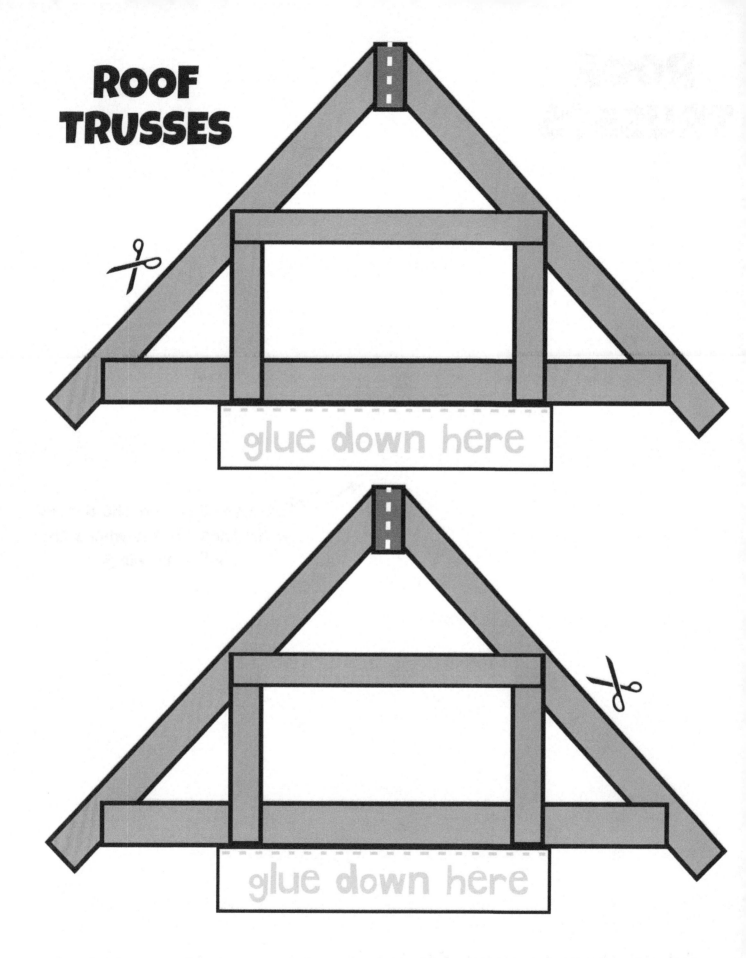

glue down here

glue down here

RIDGE BEAM

Fold on the black dotted line (same as rebar). Cut the small grey line on the tab and fold out like this. Then glue the two halves together.

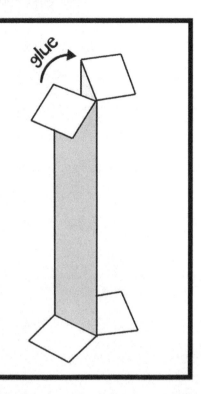

Slide the ridge beam in the truss slots.

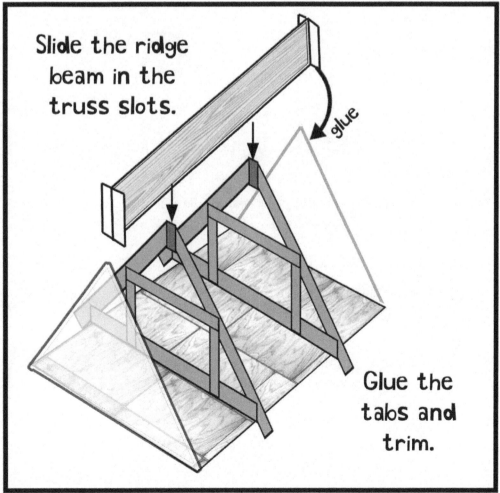

Glue the tabs and trim.

cut

cut

HOW DO YOU ATTACH THE ROOF TO THE WALL FRAME?

ANSWER

To attach the roof trusses, toenailing (nail diagonally) can be used. Or metal ties are used.

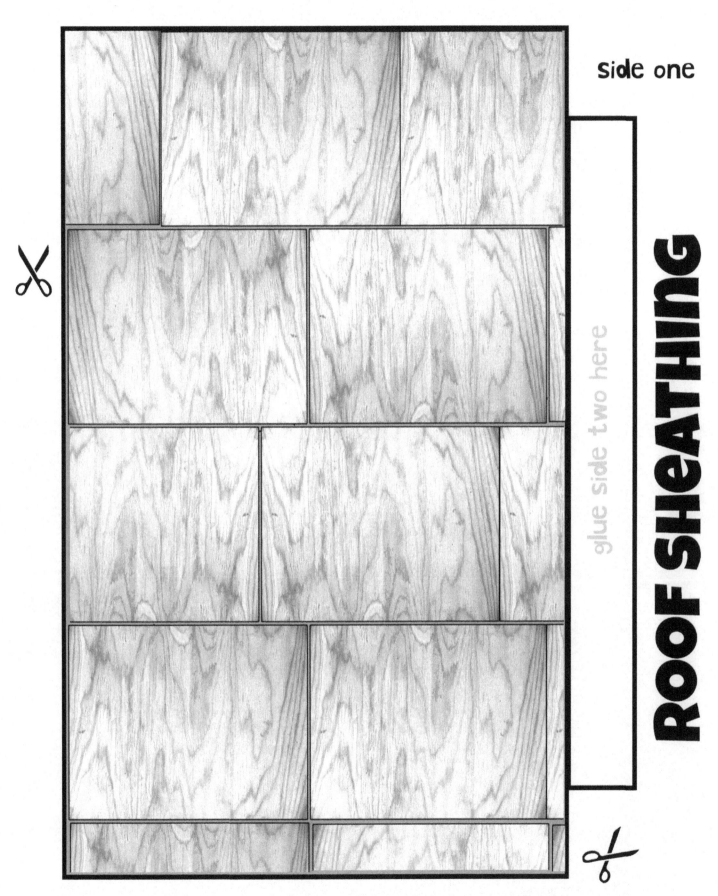

side one

glue side two here

ROOF SHEATHING

Cut out and glue both **sides** of the roof sheathing
together then only glue **side** one to the trusses.

WHAT DOES HVAC MEAN?

ANSWER

HVAC stands for heating, ventilation, air conditioning.

ROOF SHEATHING

Cut out and glue both sides of the roof sheathing
together and glue only side one to the trusses.

WHAT GOES IN FIRST? PLUMBING OR ELECTRICAL?

ANSWER

Usually plumbing. Plumbing pipes will go through framing studs.

MORE INSULATION

The attic needs insulation too. Fill in this space with paper scraps.

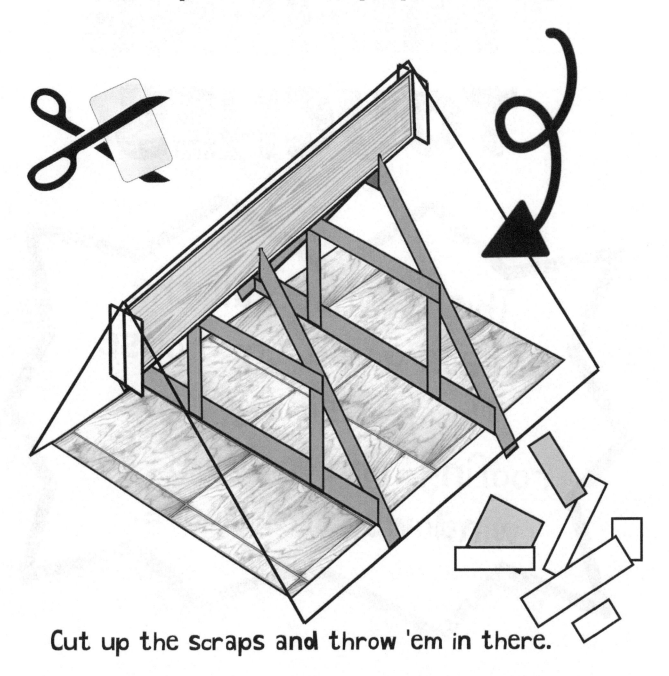

Cut up the scraps and throw 'em in there.

NOW IT'S TIME FOR THE FINISHING TOUCHES

This is where all the details go on the house, like the siding, the roofing, the molding, the windows, and doors.

PLYWOOD SHEATHING

back   front

Cut out the sheathing and glue it to the frame.

WHAT IS A VAPOR BARRIER?

ANSWER

A vapor barrier is a plastic sheet put between the drywall and studs to keep moisture out of the house.

PLYWOOD SHEATHING

left side

right side

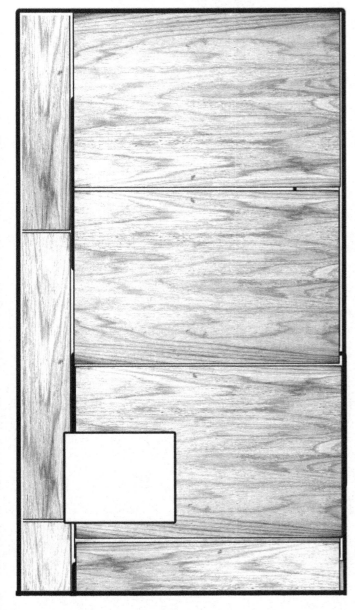
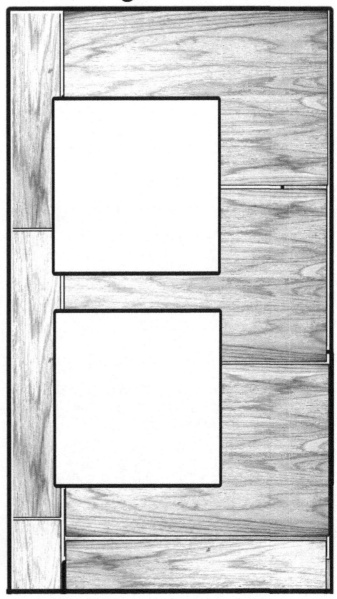

Sheathing:
The layer put on the outside of a house to attach clapboard or other exterior finishes.

WHAT IS A JOIST?

ANSWER

A joist is a long piece of wood that supports the floors and ceilings. Several will be used side by side in a house.

PLYWOOD SHEATHING

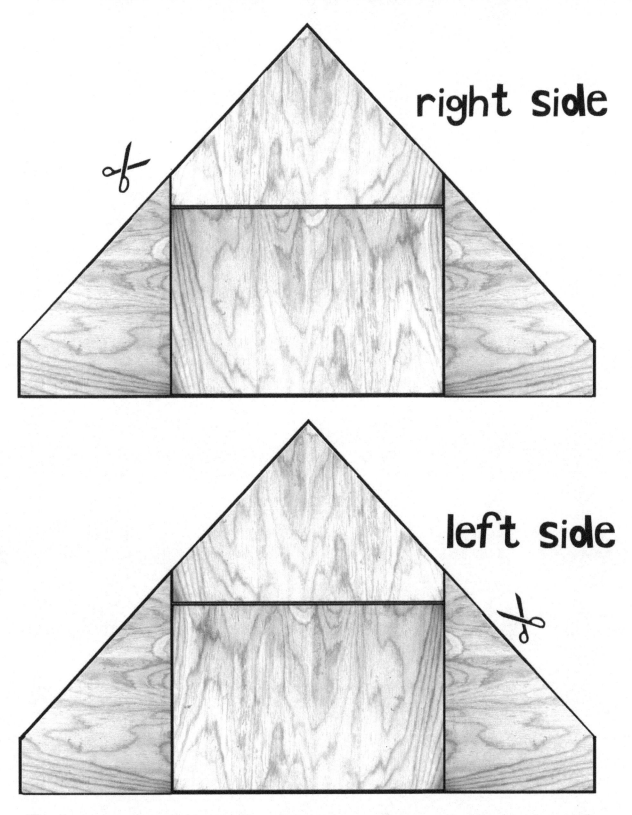

right side

left side

Cut out these triangle pieces and glue 'em to the side frame.

HOW IS A JOIST ATTACHED?

ANSWER

A joist is attached using a joist hanger (metal thingy that the joist fits into and is then nailed to a beam).

WOOD SIDING
(right side)

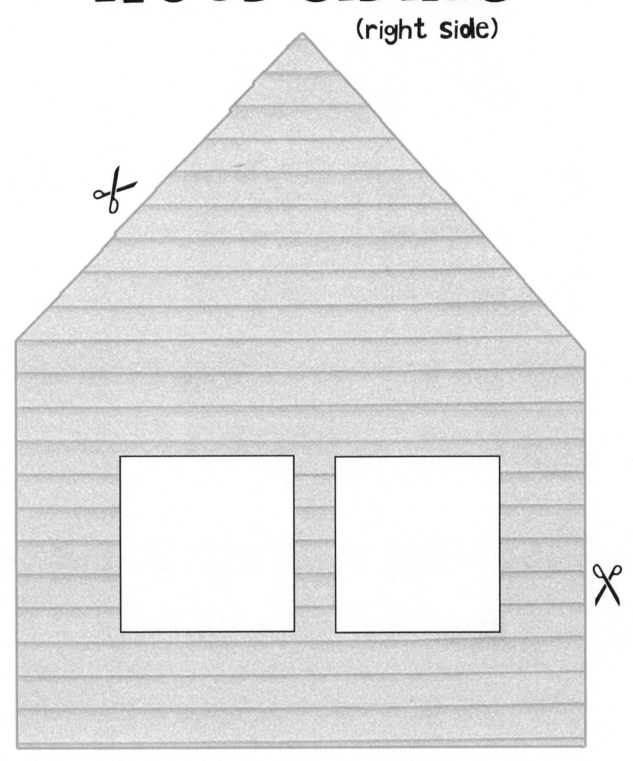

Cut out the siding and glue it to the sheathing .

WHAT IS CLADDING?

ANSWER

Cladding is the outside
skin of a building.

WOOD SIDING
(left side)

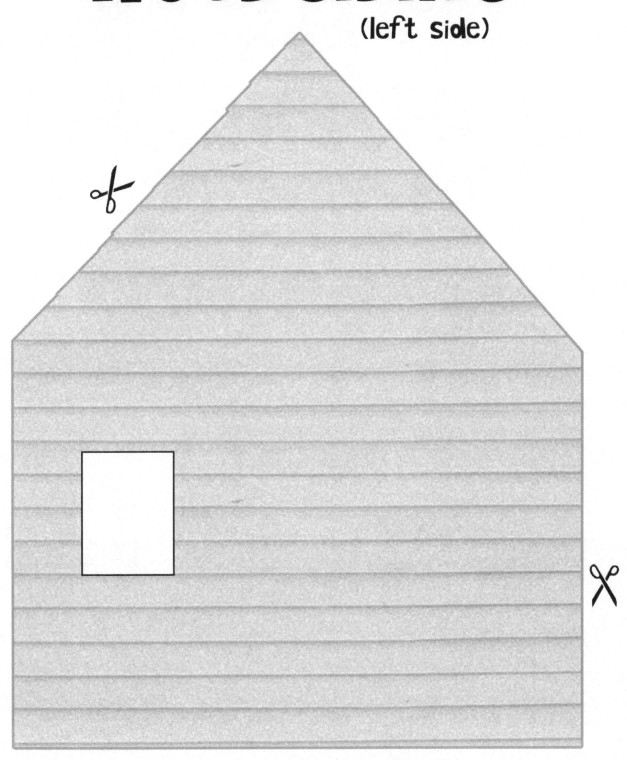

Cut out the siding and glue it to the sheathing .

WHAT ARE SOME DIFFERENT TYPES OF CLADDING?

ANSWER

Wood, stone, vinyl, metal, plaster, PVC, glass, and concrete, just to name a few.

WOOD SIDING

back   front

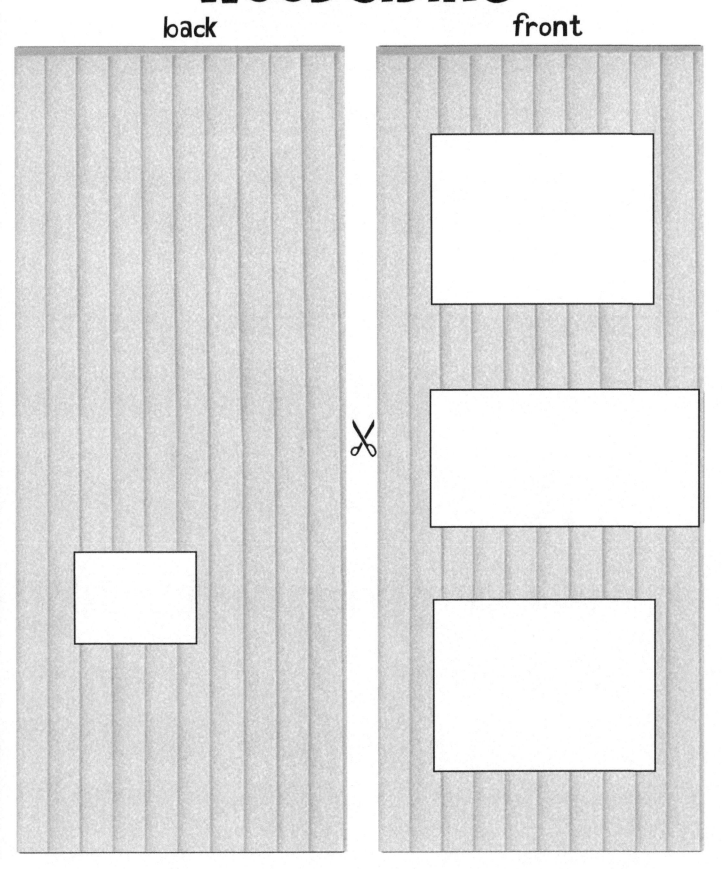

Cut out the siding and glue it to the sheathing .

WHAT IS A BATTEN?

ANSWER

A batten is a strip of wood or other material that cladding or roofing is attached to.

MOLDINGS

Color these moldings, cut 'em out, fold 'em and glue 'em to the four corners of the house as a finishing detail.

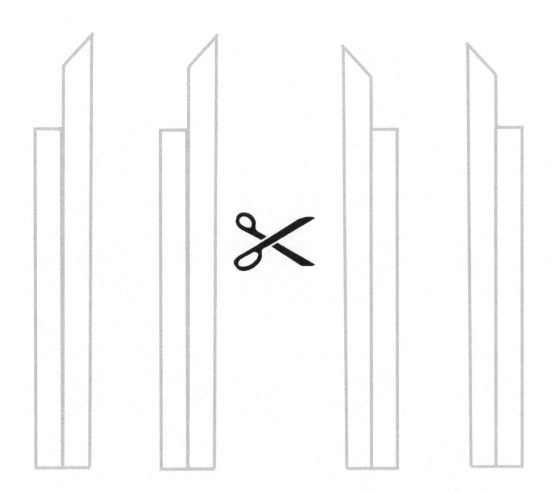

Moldings and other finishing
details will give a house clean lines.

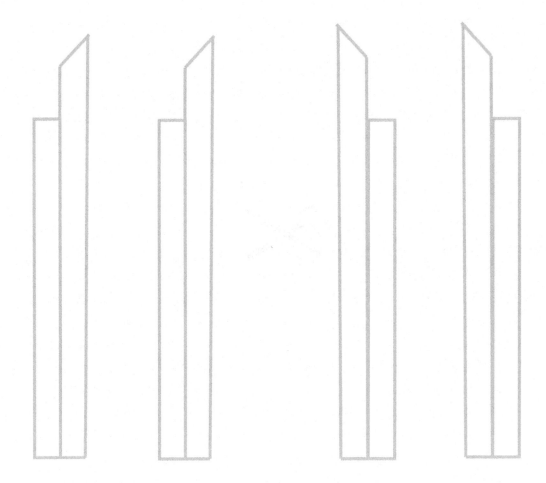

CHOOSE A ROOF STYLE

Roof finishes come in many different styles. There is, slate, thatched, concrete, asphalt shingles and in this case, paper.

ROOF CHOICES

A. Asphalt tile

B. Metal

C. Clay tile

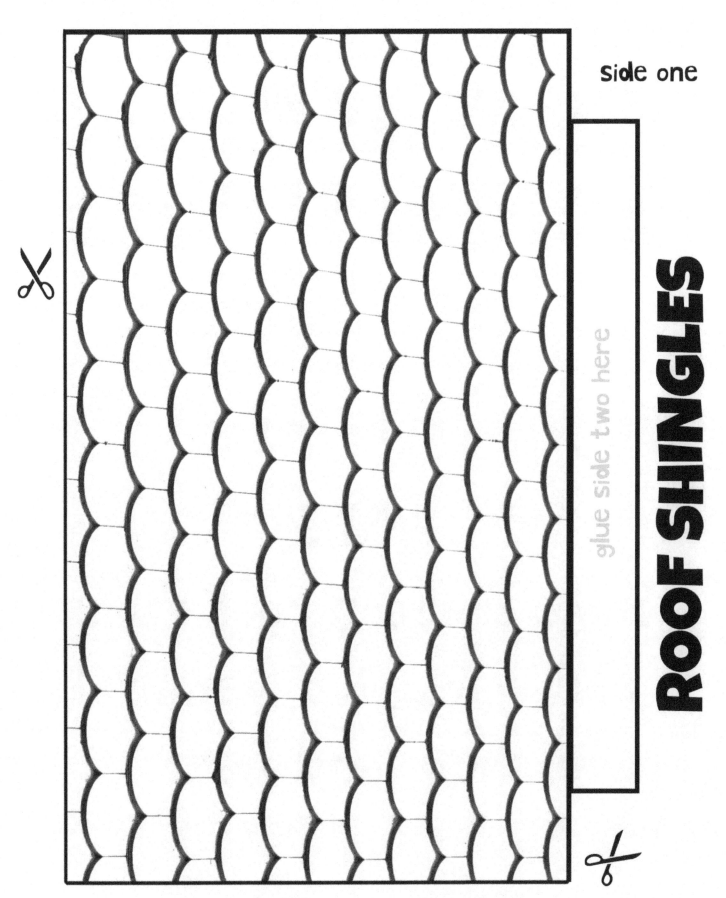

side one

ROOF SHINGLES

glue side two here

Pick a color for the roof and color.
Cut out and glue both sides of the roof shingles together.

WHAT ARE SOME COMMON ROOF STYLES?

ANSWER

Some common roof styles are: gable, hip, gambrel, shed, and flat.

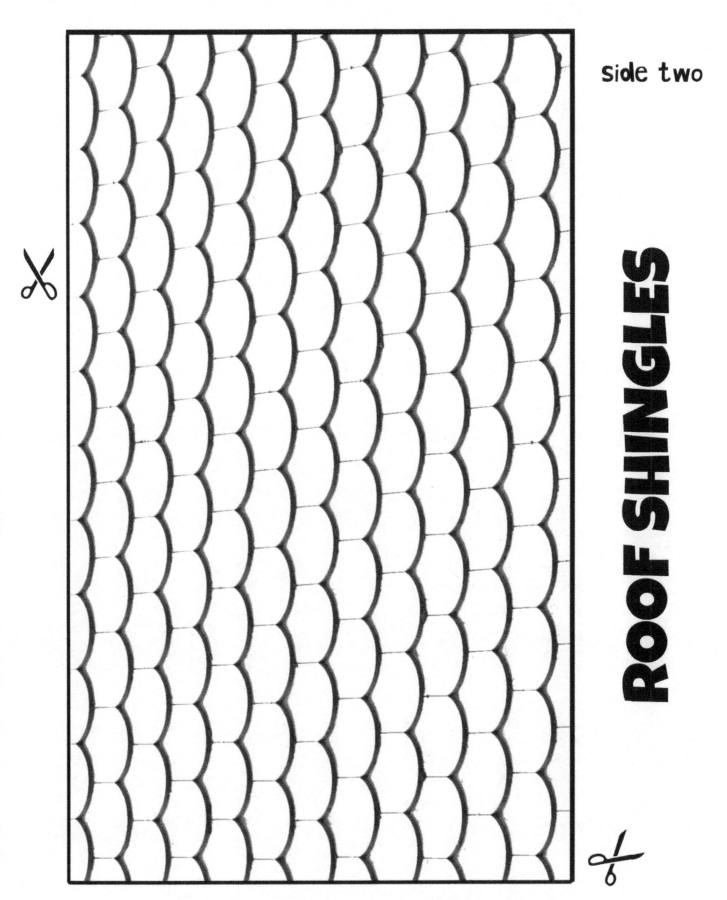

ROOF SHINGLES

Pick a color for the roof and color.
Cut out and glue both sides of the roof shingles together.

WHAT IS A DORMER?

ANSWER

A dormer is a space that sticks out from a slanted roof to give more ceiling space on the inside.

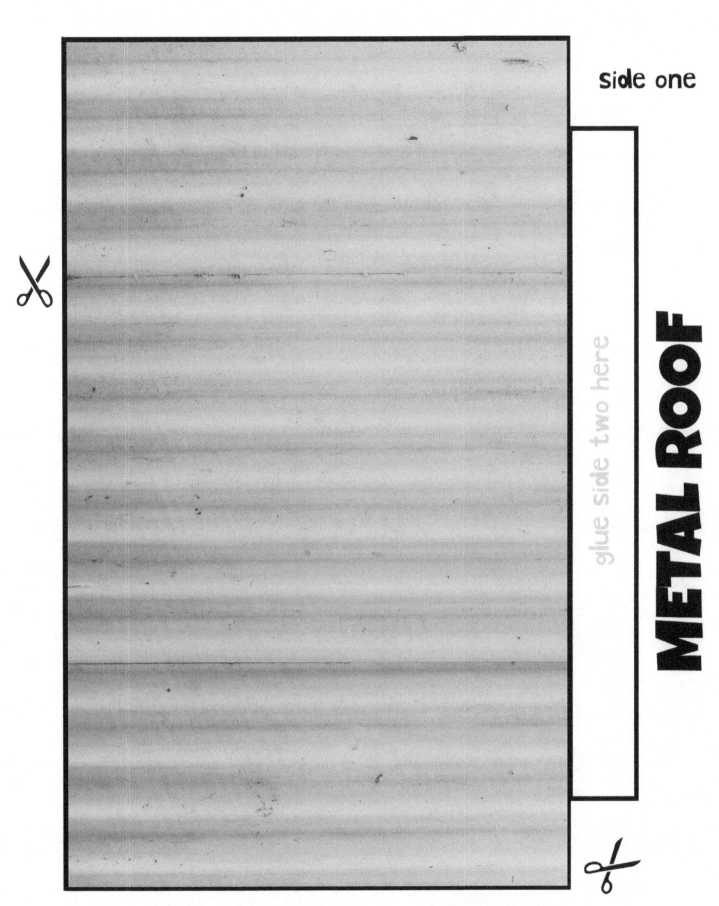

side one

glue side two here

METAL ROOF

Pick a color for the roof and color.
Cut out and glue both sides of the roof shingles together.

WHAT COSTS MORE? SHINGLES OR TILES?

ANSWER

Tiles are more expensive than shingles, however tiles will last longer.

side two

METAL ROOF

Pick a color for the roof and color.
Cut out and glue both sides of the roof shingles together.

WHAT IS A PASSIVE SOLAR HOUSE?

ANSWER

A passive solar house uses materials and techniques to naturally heat and cool a house (and saves money).

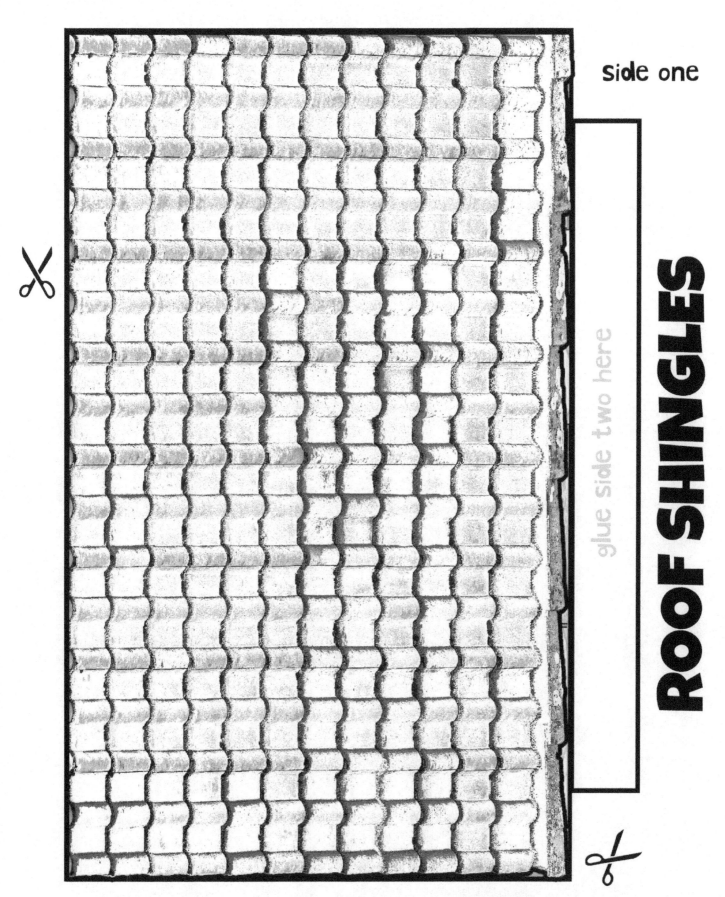

side one

ROOF SHINGLES

glue side two here

Pick a color for the roof and color.
Cut out and glue both sides of the roof shingles together.

WHAT DOES A GENERAL CONTRACTOR DO?

ANSWER

A General Contractor is the boss of a construction project. They are in charge of getting the materials, labor, equipment and manage the project schedule. THE BIG CHEESE!

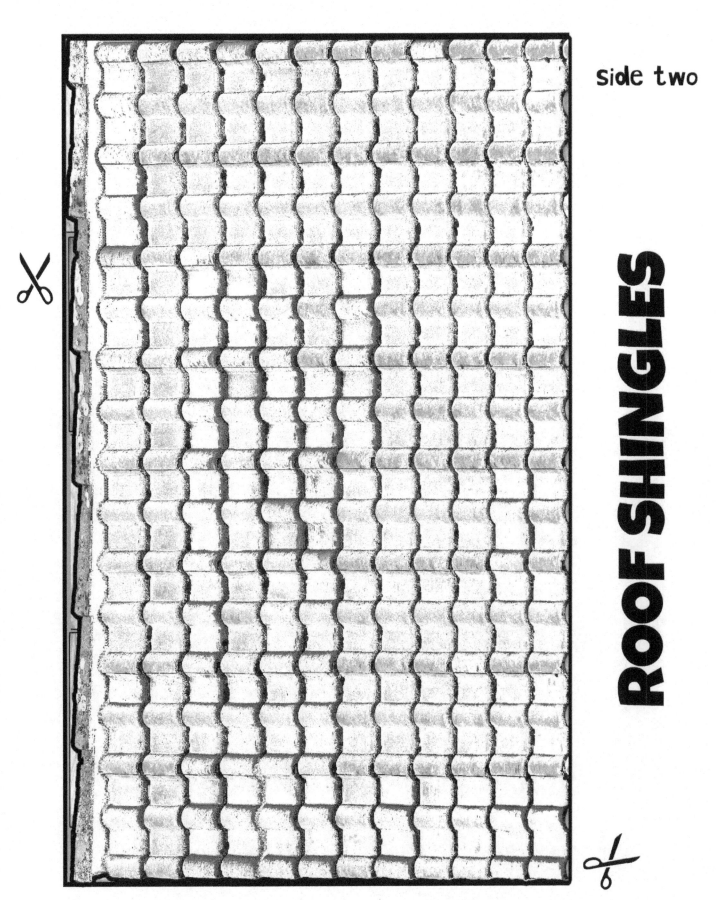

ROOF SHINGLES

Pick a color for the roof and color.
Cut out and glue both sides of the roof shingles together.

WHAT DOES AND ARCHITECT DO?

ANSWER

An Architect comes up with the design of buildings, draws them, and works with Engineers and Contractors to make sure the building is strong and looks great.

ROOF RIDGE COVERS

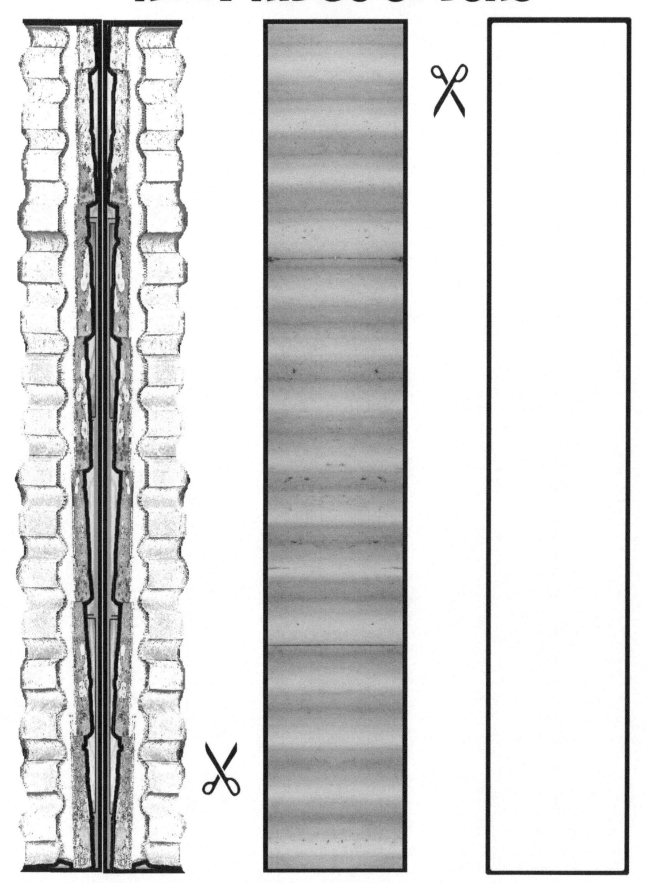

Color, cut out, fold, and glue to the top of the center of the roof.

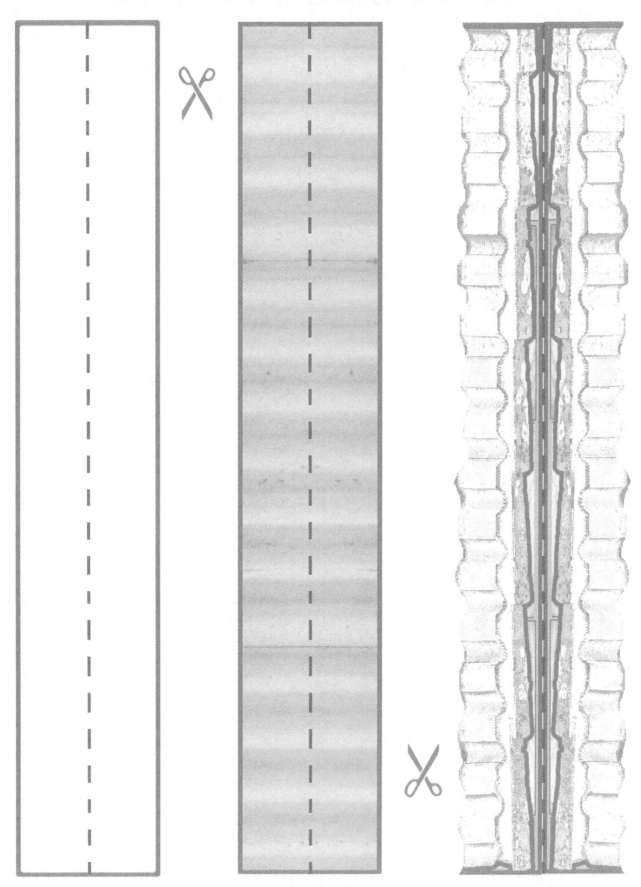

Fold on the dotted line.

FRONT DOORS

Choose a door, color it, cut it out, and stick it on.

WINDOWS

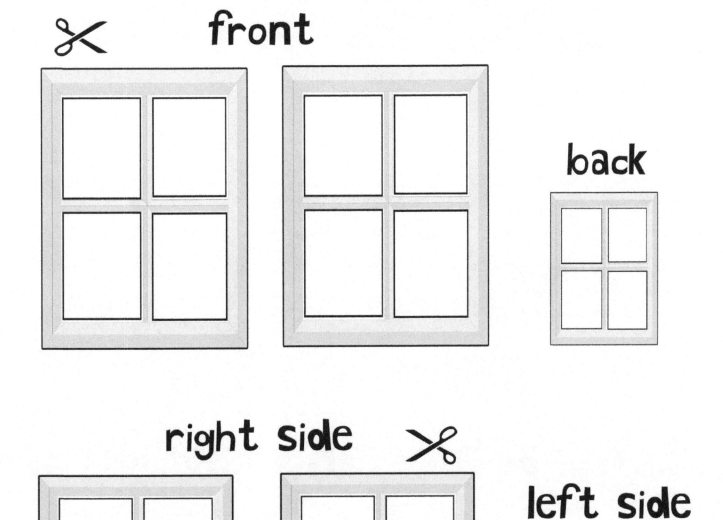

front

back

right side

left side

Color 'em, cut 'em, and stick 'em

WHAT DOES AND ENGINEER DO?

ANSWER

An Engineer works with Architects and Contractors and calculates sizes and strength of materials so structures do NOT fall down.

FIRST CLASS BUILDER

This is to certify that

Has passed everything with flying colors to become the best maker, designer, colorer, drawer, folder, logger, kid in the whole universe and is properly certified to be a:

FIRST CLASS BUILDER WITH HONORS